Treat Me Cool, Lord

Treat Me Cool, Lord

Prayers — Devotions — Litanies

*as prepared by some of God's
bad-tempered angels with
busted halos, with the help of*

Carl F. Burke

Author of *God Is for Real, Man*

28457

ASSOCIATION PRESS • NEW YORK

To Joyce

Susan

and David

Treat Me Cool, Lord

Copyright © 1968 by
National Board of Young Men's Christian Associations

Association Press, 291 Broadway, New York, N.Y. 10007

Publisher's stock numbers: 1654p, paper; 1660, cloth
Library of Congress catalog card number: 68-11493

PRINTED IN THE UNITED STATES OF AMERICA

Just bars
   And bars
      And still more bars
A hundred nights without the stars.

Just bars
   And bars
      A fence or a wall
A human life in an open stall.

The stink
   The smell
      A prison cell
Not life, a preview of hell.

                    Author unknown

Contents

Why This Book Came to Be

PRAY!

> What's the matter with you?
> You sick or something?

PRAY!

> Come off it, man!

PRAY!

> You gotta be kidding.

PRAY!

> (Dead silence)

These are reactions I'm likely to get from young people to whom I minister when I suggest that they pray. They're even more likely to laugh.

Praying, for many of these young people, is a "real waste of time." Traditional "prayer talk" is a foreign language to them, meaningless words that they may encounter in the King James Version of the Bible or in a hymnal, but nowhere else.

For one brief period, in an effort to see whether written prayers would be meaningful to them, I asked some of them to put the prayers in their own words. This material, from books of prayers and from hymnals, was rejected. The young people have no background of religious training, but the prayers presupposed that readers had established a mature relationship with God.

Many of the words used in the "prepared" prayers have no meaning for them—words such as "wast," "dost," and "quickened." Indeed, their experience with these prayers was much like that of speaking a new language. Sometimes they called it "the God talk" or "the Jesus bit." Many of the prayers use cliches that have meaning, perhaps, for the churchgoer (though sometimes I question that) but that do not relate to the problems and lives of these children and young people. Examples are: "Grant now thy grace," "the upper room," "in whom we live and move and have our being," and "Do thou grant us."

Kenneth L. Wilson has made a similar point:

> While we feel comfortable with a "wilt not," it gets a bit sticky if we have to cope with a "goest" or "leavest." And though it may be simply a personal aversion, I must admit that I have always dragged my feet a bit at the preface, "Do thou grant us..." One is never sure whether it's a command, a request, or a question. "Didst" is another word that seems to be a futile

attempt to gild the lily. "As thy Son didst walk this earth" does not seem to be nearly as eloquent or even as devout as would be "As your Son walked . . ." or better yet, "As your Son shared our human experience."[1]

For youth in trouble, prayer in this kind of language has no relationship to the real "gut issues of life." Instead, it pertains only to the unreal world of a church visited on the occasion of a funeral or a wedding, if at all.

Yet if we believe that prayer grows out of deep human need, out of the real world, out of the confrontation of daily situations, these children and young people surely need prayer. As Kenneth Wilson has said, "Inability to pray certainly doesn't stem from having nothing to say. Often it does stem from not knowing how to say it."[2]

To help these boys and girls learn to pray, I have worked with them over a period of years in the phrasing of prayers in their own language. It has been a frustrating task frequently for a minister with seventeen years of training and experience to discover that he is still unable to communicate even basic Christian concepts to a boy or a girl to whom he is called to minister.

The problem is more than one of semantics. It involves cultural concepts, family relation-

[1]Kenneth L. Wilson, "Land of the Wasts and Dosts," *Christian Herald, June, 1966, pp. 24-25.* Copyrighted by *Christian Herald;* used by permission.
[2]*Ibid.*

ships, and social problems of every description—actually, total value systems.

A person who intends to do this kind of work with disadvantaged young people and children must realize that he is a phony in their eyes. This barrier is very difficult to overcome. Most of the experiences these boys and girls have had with adults have been with parents who have rejected them, with social workers who consider them difficult cases, or with practice teachers administering some kind of test for use in making a report to a university class. "Here's another creep" is the youths' attitude.

The person with the ready answers will be quickly rejected. It may take several years of building one's reputation with the children to overcome the barriers; with some of them it will never be achieved. Probably nothing helpful can be achieved until the confidence of the children has been won.

It must also be recognized that not every session with a youngster has to be "productive." Middle-class goals of success are not their goals, and the feeling of failure on an adult's part may become a barrier. Further, we need to realize that we are not trying to teach middle-class goals and that prayer speaks for itself. Another important principle is the fact that anything can be used as a starting point; the adult must be alert to the proper time to begin guiding the conversation.

Another factor is the degree to which the adult can adjust to shock. Disadvantaged youth may try many methods of shocking middle-class adults just to see them squirm. It would be helpful to know something of the reasons why we are shocked by speech patterns and values other than our own. There are, of course, many psychological factors, but the most important one is that the children learn to trust us and that we trust them. Christian learning cannot be forced with these children; it must be natural and arise out of a natural situation.

But this book is not a textbook of methodology. It presents a collection of prayers by children and young people gathered over a period of years in jail, in detention homes for boys and girls, in summer camps for disadvantaged youth. They are recorded with little change, except for spelling corrections, from their original expression by the youngsters. Most of the prayers are brief, and the words are simple, reflecting the backgrounds of the authors, many of whom were school dropouts and often suffering emotional and social disturbances of varying degree. Often their word comprehension was on the second- or third-grade level, although their ages ranged from ten to seventeen. Their prayers show that they have been hurt by problems with which they cannot cope. They reveal that the majority of youngsters are from a culture different from that known to most of us.

Words no longer "in" may be found in the book; slang and street talk change almost daily, even from one street to the next and from one age group to another.

There are some similarities between the prayers, reflecting the common problems of the authors. I encouraged the boys and girls to express their real feelings to God. Sometimes the prayers grew out of an exchange of ideas that came to the surface in conversation. At other times a prayer expressed a wish that God would correct a certain situation. Some of the prayers developed in small groups. A few are paraphrases of familiar prayers and collects; some are from the Psalms.

As illustrations of how these prayers can be used in formal worship sessions, I have added a few outlines of worship services in jail.

It is my hope that these prayers will reveal insights into the real feeling and experiences of others as they call upon God for help. Perhaps some will find this book offensive and the language of the prayers distasteful. I can only defend this from the viewpoint that words, thought patterns, and frames of reference are not the important aspects of prayer. It is the feelings and the concerns being expressed that our Lord hears.

CARL F. BURKE
Chaplain, Erie County Jail
Buffalo, New York

Prayers

The following are examples of prayers composed by young people ten through seventeen years of age. You may be startled with the language, the brevity, and the straightforwardness of most of these prayers, but who can doubt their sincerity?

In many cases the author was prompting or counseling the young person to face his problems and express his true feelings to God.

To be sure, humor is found here...and pathos ...and pity. But there is also faith—perhaps a "childlike faith"—and at least a start on the long trail that leads to trust and dependence on God and to acceptance of the Christian way of life.

No doubt the most startling prayer of all was uttered at an evening campfire at Camp Vick, the Western New York Baptist Camp, during the Junior Citizens' Camp. An eleven-year-old boy had asked if he could "say the prayer" at the end of the program and been given permission. It was his prayer that is in part responsible for this book. Here it is:

> Dear Lord, we thank you for giving us
> one hell of a good time today.

The sincerity of the prayer was felt so strongly that nobody laughed.

For Kids Stretched Out

Sometimes things don't go so good,
God, for kids we know
Maybe at their crib
Or maybe they is just loose
Or flagged out at school.

We hope you can pick them up
Before they get down too far
And they punt out too soon.

It's easy to do
So we need someone to
Really turn us on.

Alone

There is no use
Giving a snow job to you, Lord.
You already know me like a book.

So when I'm all alone
Help me to see me like I am
Even if I don't like it.

Inside of me I want the right thing
Then when I'm with someone
I want them to think I'm the big man.

When I'm all alone tonight, God,
Help me see
What you want me to be like.

Watch Us Good

'Fore we go to sleep
We say a prayer
So you watch us good.

We is sorry
For fights and swearing
And any stealing and sins
That you don't like.

We ask you
Don't leave us when we sleep
And forget about our sins,
And we'll do the same.

Sentence Prayers

Thank you for Christmas
And what the Salvation Army did.

* * *

Lord, we sure enough need
Someone to keep us from
Being scared
To get called chicken.

* * *

God, why is we always willing
To hate the fuz—when most
Of the time they ain't that bad?

* * *

For all the sins we did
And might did in a few days
We is sorry.

* * *

Please make Papa stay away from the gin mill.

* * *

The prayer of a narcotic addict:

O my God, why did I ever start this?...
Please, Jesus, help me to let go.

* * *

Unfortunately some of the prayers in a jail come under the title "I've heard that before":

Dear God, If I get out of this
I'll never get into trouble again.

(Heard often before the judge passes sentence)

One inmate dryly remarked, "I suppose God looks down and says, 'So, what else is new?'"

I Pray for Me

God, I pray for me
Mostly when I need you.
Help me think of you
When I'm not busted
Then maybe I won't
Get busted.

All By Myself

O God, I'm alone.
It's hard to feel that anyone cares,
Including you, O God.

I wonder if anyone understands
My wanting a friend
Who don't want nothing from me.

Help me to believe
You are my friend
And to know
You are with me.

Keep me from making a fool of myself.

I don't want to become bitter
And filled with hate—
I've seen too much hate

I don't want to be angry anymore.

Forgive me, please,
For what I have done,
And help me live right again.

I pray, wondering if you hear me.

Help Us Knock It Off

These dirty words we say
We don't mean it bad
They just come out
Mostly when we is mad
Sorry about that!

Dear God—
Your law says no swearing—
Man! Did we ever bust that law!

Sometimes we try not to do it—
Try real hard too!
But we do it anyway.
We sure hope
You'll help us
To knock it off.

Help Me to Get Up

God, I tried hard to make it—
Maybe too hard.
Now I'm down again
Help me to get up.

I'm sorry—
But not sure what that means.

I'm ashamed—
But not sure of what.

I'm not sure of many things
Like
Your love
And care
Or if you even exist.

Something inside of me
Keeps telling me you do.
Dear God, help me to believe
And to act like I do.

Help Me Say the Right Thing

The kid
Thinks he's the big man.

I know he's just a punk.

Too many people listen to him
Blow off his mouth.

God, if only I could say
The right thing.

I don't want to hurt him.
He never had
So many people
Listen to him before.

God, help me say
The right thing
Before more people
Get hurt.

The Bottle

So who cares?
I don't.

If I do care
It makes me forget.

But I hate it—
And myself—
And I want to care.

That's sort of mixed up, Lord.
Is that why I go
Back to the Bottle?

It Ain't Funny

My dad's a drunk, Lord,
And some people
Think it's funny.

Why do they do that
When it ain't funny at all?

Help Him, Lord

There is this here kid
Who is always sick.
You healed people before.
Maybe you could
Do it again for him.
If you can, God,
We'll help
Take care of him
For you.

Remember Mom

Dear God—My mom tries
Awful hard to help us kids.
But she don't feel so good
Lots of times.
They say you care
About sick people—
Hope you remember Mom.

He Ain't Funny

Dear Jesus—
We got a retard
In our apartment house
The kids mock him out
And think he is funny.
Help us to think he ain't funny.

We're Glad

We're glad to have you around, God,
And to love you
And try to follow you.

We're glad to know that you are great
And you always remember us—
Even if
We don't you.

We hope you will
Help us come clean, God,
So we can see you,
Or anyway
Know you know us.

It Ain't Changed

They tell me to "get with it"
But I only give up—
I'm even scared to look at you.
So what if a new day comes
It's always the same.
Don't blame me, God,
If it all seems
Like there is no hope!

People talk about beauty—
In an alley?

They talk about love—
In a bar?

They talk about providing—
You ever been without a job?

They talk about truth—
Where is it?

They tell me turn to you,
I did—
But it's still the same.

The Wall

What does it do, Lord—
Keep us in?
Keep others out?

Why do we build a fence—
To keep ourself in
Or you out?

Forgive us, we ask—
For building walls!

God's Presence

We're glad we can think
You are a father
Maybe like we wish we got.

We are happy
That you will stay around.
Just thinking about that
Makes us feel just great.

Uncertainty

We wish we were sure
About you, God.
We want to believe—
But it's kinda hard.

Mostly hard to pray, Lord.
Kinda gives you the
Creeps to pray
And not be sure
Anyone's hearing.

Facing Up to Life

When we can't take it anymore
And want to run away—
And just run
And run
And run
Help us to face our problem
And find a way to beat it.

I tried so hard
And I don't know
Why it didn't work
I'm sure I believe in you.

Why?

Dear God—
Why do religious people
Always know they
Are so right
When they don't give
Us a chance to talk?

We Want Friends

Dear Lord—help us to be like you
And do what's right.
Keep us from thinking rotten
Things about people
But make a friend outta them.

Make our friends and us for real
Help us say good things about others
And not mock out people.

Helpfulness

We want to do something real good—
Like helping other kids
Or making homes better
Or giving someone a break
Or helping someone not
To feel sorry for himself
Or from giving up
Or from shoplifting
Or from snatching a purse,
But mostly to keep them out of trouble
And don't forget to love 'em
Even if we can't help them, Jesus.

Scared

God—
I'm scared
I feel funny
On my insides
I wish you wus here.

Maybe if I could help somebody
I'd feel better on the insides
Just doing one good thing
For a change—
Help me do it, God.

Searching

Do you know what it is like
To search for someone to love
And never find someone?

Why, O God,
Did it take this
To make me
Find myself?

Where have you been?
Where have I been?
Is it too late for me?
Is there still a chance?

Sinfulness

Make us
Hate sin
So much, Lord,
We won't have
Nothin' to do
With it.
We mean it!

Fighting

All this climbing up
On people gets me
In a mess.
Wontcha help me
Knock it off?

But I ain't gonna
Let anybody climb up on me
So I guess you just gotta
Do something about it.

How Come, God?

How come it's hard to think of you
And to think you around us?
They is gotta be an answer.

How come we don't think about
What we is supposed to do?

How come so many people
Mock you out?

How come you don't get them, God,
And fix 'em good?

How come things get so
Mixed up?

How come things is
Such a mess?

How come it's so hard
To believe in you?

What's "In" and "Out"

Jesus, help us to live for you.
So we are asking you
To show us what things is OK
And what things is out for us.

Help us to get dirty thoughts
Out of our mind
Then with them things out
We hope you will be in.

Thanks for Being a Friend

When we need a friend
Thanks 'cause you're there.
We hope we're a friend of yours.

Thanks for giving us a few.
Most of them is pretty good,
But sometimes they ain't so hot.

We hope we can help them
And you will stick with us.
Thanks for being a friend.

Sometimes

Sometimes, dear Jesus, we wish
Everything was cleaner
And not so dirty.

Sometimes we wish
We was real strong
When people bug us.

Sometimes we wish
We was true when we is
Scared of the big kids.

Sometimes we wish
We had
A bigger house.

Sometimes we wish
You were around here
More often, Jesus.

Right Things

God, you know we want to do the right things
But what's the use?
Most of the time
Nothing goes right anyway.

So we hope you'll understand
If we say what's the use?

That don't mean
We like it that way
And we hope
We can get it changed.

We Wanta Do Good

God, help us think up good things to do—
Like helping kids what needs help
Or maybe like helping old ladies.
Inside we don't really like
Just doin' nothing
And getting people mad at us.
Maybe it would give us a
Good feeling about you, God,
If you could help us.

Changes

God, seems like nothing stays still
People always movin' in and out
New teaches most every week
Even different cops in the fuz wagon
Hope you don't change things
Too much, God.

Help the Inside Win

God, we try hard in school, sometimes,
Inside we want to make it
Outside what's the use?
So we hope you get around
To helpin' the inside win.

Listening

God, help us to listen to the teach today
'Cause we don't got to go noplace.
Maybe something she got to say is
Gonna help us.

We Tries

God, guess we better get around
To doing what you say we should.
Only sometimes the way your laws is
In the Bible gets us all mixed up.
Seems like nobody around here
Believes them except the preacher,
And nobody seems to pay him much attention.
So what do you expect of us?
Don't mean that nasty-like,
But we does try sometimes.

Help Us Care

God, I guess we care more about the kids
Around us than we do
About other people and about you.

God, I guess we need to fix that up,
So can we count on you for help?

Forgive ... ?

People tell us you will forgive us.
We don't worry about you doing it,
God, but what about people
Like cops, and teachers,
And caseworkers, and preachers.
Don't they s'pose to do it too?
So we hope you'll help them too.

Rotten Things

God, when we want to do rotten things,
Show us how to wait up for you
And to care about other people.

God, when we don't want
To do what we is suppose to do,
Help us to care about you.

We Need Help

God, we need all the help we can get today.
We ain't going to do much
Unless we get it from you.

So we needs lots of guts
To live like we should.

We need to think about
How someone feels when
We mock them out.

We need your help
So we won't get stupid ideas
And stuff like that.

Getting Mad

God, we get mad too quick
And blow our top
And get people mad at us.

We need you to help us
Build up a real cool.

Sometimes we think we
Got things all figured out
About other people.

We need your help to believe
They only wants to help us.

Talking

Dear Jesus, we hear lots of people
Talking about you
But we don't get to see you
And most of the people
Talking about you
Don't know much
About the troubles we got,
So we hope you do.

They is always talking about
Saving us from sin
And other dirty stuff.
We don't know
How you going to do it
But thanks anyway.

Questions

People always telling us
You is the answer
But we didn't ask them
Any questions.

You may be the answer, Jesus,
But I hope you know how we all feel,
And anyway I don't think
The people up in that church
Care much about us.

We don't about them anyway.
But I guess that we want them to,
So maybe they is the ones
That need your help
More than we do.

Fix Up Our Brains

Dear God, how about fixin' up our brains
To think good things about other kids
'Stead of ways to beat the hell out of them?
We want people to like us.
How about us liking other kids?

Stick Up for Us

God, don't you know I needs some help?
We need you to stick up for us and
Keep us from getting hurt
And from always thinking awful rotten things.

Stick Around, God

Dear God, help us to make a plan
Like your son did.
Help us stick up
For the right things
And do the right things and stuff—
Things like liking the right stuff
And going around
With the right kind of kids—
You know the kind you like.

Runnin'

We is always runnin' like we was crazy-like
Most of the time anyway
We ain't going nowhere
And we need to cool it
So we can talk to you, God.

Sometimes, God,
We ain't seen no good to do.

Sometimes, God,
We wish we had something good to do
'Stead of just hanging around.

God, when I'm in a mess but good
And I wanta get real boss
And stand up tall
Gimme the word, God,
And help me to level with you.

Give Us a Lift

Dear God, we gotta get a lift from you
'Cause we can't do it ourselves
And neither can anybody else—
Only you.

We need a little more guts
In fact lots more
And a little more push
To do what we s'pose to do.

We need to give the other guy a break
And think about how he feels
And even to put up with him
Even if we don't like it.

We gotta get help from you
So we won't quit so easy
So when we get older
We got something.

We ask you to help us
Keep away from stupid ideas
And do what's right
Even if it is hard.

Then we know that
Everything will be real boss.

Do You Really Care?

Dear Lord,
People always telling me
About poor heathen
And how you love them,
But sometimes I don't think
You even care about me,
Never mind them.

They is lots of poor people
Who needs help
And they gets the same idea
About you that I do, too.
It's that I guess you is too busy
With lots of things
To take a look at me. Don't worry about it
'Cause we'll get along somehow and
Make it in our own way.

I guess that we really do
Want you to take a look at us and
I guess that we really do
Want it easy to believe in you,
'Cause it's kind of hard right now.

Trust

They tell us we suppose to trust you
But most of the time we don't
And sometimes you seem like only a word
That don't mean nothing.

Most of the time we want to trust
Someone but we ain't sure we can and
That's sure true when we are in trouble.
Sometimes we don't even trust ourself
And that gets us mixed up too.

So, God, can you help us
When we're all mixed up?
Sometimes people give us a snow job,
And try to say that
Everything is gonna come out alright,
But most of the time that it don't.

So we don't need
No more of that kind of help.
Just level with us, God,
And it will help a lot.

Help Them to Know We Ain't All Bad

Dear God, people are always buggin' us
To be something better.
They do lots of preaching.
Sometimes it makes sense
And sometimes it just
Don't come out right and
We feel that they just don't know
What they are talking about.
We ask you to help them
To know that we ain't all bad.
Help them to know that we want
To do the right thing
But sometimes what's the use?

Help Me Take It

Dear God, You already know
That I didn't want it to happen.
I guess I knew that I'd get hit anyway.
Help me to take it without showing
How lame I am in this stuff.

This bit may not seem
Like much at first,
But I guess that it really is.
Help me to get stronger from it.

I know that it's going too rough,
But please, God,
Don't let me get any madder at people
Than I already am.

Then the Cell Door Bangs Shut

Now, Lord, I'm all alone—
Just the two of us here
I always wanted time to think.

In this lonely
And scary place
Help me to find
Myself
And you.

Lead my thoughts
Here by myself and you
In my mind
In my heart
In my life.

When the lights are out
And it's quiet
May I hear your voice
Speaking to me
Showing me the right way.

Gettin' to Know God

God, sometimes you seem so far away we
wonder if we can ever know what you are like.
Help us to get to know you better so we can
believe you made us. We ask you to help us get
rid of all our sins so that we can get to know you.

A Time to Pray

Oh, Father,
It's time to pray
And ask you to forgive our sin
In the name
Of the Father
Son
And Holy Ghost.

Shoplifting

Dear God, I'm only thirteen years old. I'm all mixed up and don't know where to turn. My friends tell me it's alright to shoplift and that it's a good way to get lots of stuff that I just ain't got now. I tried it and it sure felt good to have those stockings and a nice new blouse for a change.

Inside of me I guess I know it's wrong to do this, but it seems like all my friends are doing it and that gets me all mixed up. Now I don't dare tell my folks and I don't dare to back off on account they'll call me chicken and we don't like that either. When I do wrong things I really do feel bad inside and I guess I want someone to say that you are forgiven and more than that, Lord, I guess I do want someone to help me stop this.

So I ask you to help me see what I'm getting into and for the courage to stop and say no to the others and mean it. So I do ask for forgiveness and for courage to do what I already know I should do.

Forgive and Help Us

Oh, heavenly Father,
I am down on my knee
Asking my heavenly Father if he would
Forgive me for what I did.
Oh, heavenly Father,
Help me do what's right
And not what's bad.

        *   *   *

My dearest Father,
I need you to help me,
To forgive my sin
And help my mother
And father
And sisters
Do what's right
In your eye.

        *   *   *

My dearest Father,
I believe in your name
And in you.

        *   *   *

Dearest Father, forgive us for our sin.

I Love You

I love you
Oh, heavenly Father, I love you
I only believe in one God
And I know everyone loves you like I do
For all you have did—
And believes in you—
And we know that you
Will help us with our sin.

We're Mighty Glad

Thanks, God, that we can call you father. Sometimes we don't know for sure what that means, but just like we think of a father should treat you we hope you will treat us. We are thankful that even though parents may walk out on you, you never will. We are mighty glad to know that you are around all the time to help us make a go of life. On account of you're a good father we hope we can serve you all the time.

Our Own Two Feets

Lord, we know you s'pose to guide us with your
  hand
But we don't let you put a finger on us.
We know you s'pose to guide us with your eye
But we stay outta your sight,
That you s'pose to be with us all the time
But we make believe you ain't here,
That you can teach us right from wrong
But we ain't listenin' to you
Even though you know best.

Please God, help us to be strong
And stand up for good things
On our own two feets
And make up our minds by our own selves
And most of all to listen to you
And pay attention to you.
'Cause Jesus said so.

Send Him By

Dear God, The preacher man says you s'pose to send a Holy Spirit to stay with us and help us in trouble, which we got plenty of. But we don't seen him yet.

We sure need him now. The preacher says that he s'pose to go up and down the earth but I guess that he ain't got here yet.

So when we pray, we askin' you to send him by this place and lend us a hand.

About Being Dumb

Dear God, We been awful dumb
And turned around on you.
We been awful deaf, too.
'Cause we didn't hear
What your son been saying.
We been following the bunch we travel with.

Sometimes we are all fulled up with scary things
Sometimes we just don't know enough about
　　　things
Sometimes we just want lots of things
Like when we afraid someone else
Will get before we do.
Sometimes we got the wrong ideas about people
Just 'cause they is different from us.

We don't like this kind of stuff
And we need some help from you to change it.

Trouble

You gave us the world, God,
We hope we can take care of it
But sometimes seems like we don't do so good.

There is all kinds of trouble, God,
We hope we can do something to help people
Who got lots of trouble.

The Bible says that you gave us talents.
We hope that we can use them in a good way.

A Crowd

Dear God, If there's one thing
I don't need it's more people around me.
Seems like everybody is always watching me.

We need some time to think things over.
Hope you will give it to us.
And we need time to figure out what's happened
    to us.

Is it a sin, God,
To want people to leave you alone?

Some Rich, Some Poor

Why did you make some rich people
And some poor people?
Why did I have to be a poor one?
If only we could have a couple of nice things.
And a few good days too!

And I Want to, Too!

Dear God, The time has come to go home and I'm scared mostly 'cause I want things to go right this time. Everybody is tellin' me how I just got to do better in school and I want to. They tellin' me I just gotta obey my mother, and I want to, they tellin' me I just gotta listen to my worker and I want to, they just tellin' me all kinds of things that I just gotta do. Maybe I just gotta listen to you, too, God, so I hope that you will help me.

Helpin' You!

Oh God in heaven,
Help us to remember kids who need you
Some who are hungry
Some who got parents who don't give a damn
    about them
And the ones who get called nigger and dago
Some who ain't got nobody who cares about
    them.

When the parents are at the gin mill
And the little kids is crying
Help us to love them.

When the black kids get called nigger
Help us to stick up for them.

We hope we don't get tired
Doing the things we suppose to do
To help other people
'Cause we s'pose to help you.

Show Me How

Dear God—Thanks a lot
For good things you give us
For the schoolteachers that like us
The preacher who's our friend,
For mothers who try so hard.

Dear God—
Help me then to think of other kids
And to work hard
And to get the right ideas.

Dear God—
They is kids that I know
That needs all kinds of help
And food
And friends.
Maybe I can help them.
I hope you will show me how.

Christmas

Christmas is all over now, God.
So what will happen now?
Most everybody says, "God! That's over with."
I guess that they don't know what it means.

So, God, help us guys to remember
That you sent Jesus to see us.

Then maybe we will remember
To treat people like they really was somebody
Everyday and not just on Christmas.

Tied Up

Jesus, I want to say lots of things to you
And tell you how I feel
But I don't see you
And it feels kinda silly
Talking to someone you don't see.

I'm kinda all tied up inside of me
And here's a hope you will help me
Get untied.

I'm even afraid that somebody is going to
Laugh at me and poke fun at me
And call me some kind of a creep.
I wished I could feel that I could
Trust you.

Those Dirty Things We Did

Dear God and Jesus—
Man, have we said some dirty things about other
        people
And done some rotten things.
Lots of them we don't even want to talk about.

We ask you to forgive us what we said
And what we done did.
We want lots of friends,
But we don't let them be our friend
Mostly 'cause we say dirty things about them
And we don't even know why.
So we is sorry, God.

Prayer for Good Friday

His face looks bashed in, God,
His clothes is all torn and taken away from him,
His body is stuck.
How come, God?
Don't seem like you had to rough him up like
    that.

Slow Down . . . Cool It

Make us slow down and cool it but good, God,
So we can get with it.
We need to find out where we is going
To find out how to be happy
And do good things.
We want to be a good guy and in a way we don't.
Mostly 'cause we don't see any point in it.
What's it going to get us is what we ask you.
What's the use if you still live in a dump
And all that happens is you get beat up?
These is the things we ask you.

Hang Around, God

God, we ain't so strong
And get scared easy—
We hope you will
Hang around with us
So we won't get scared
And get bad ideas
Or get hurt.

Thinking With Everything

Dear God, make me think about what I'm doing
With my mind
With my body
With my habits
With my study
With my friends
With my hopes
With my parents
With my faith
With life.

For Kids Everyplace

We pray for kids
Everyplace in the whole world,
You bet we do.
Some got no houses
Some is got no food
And some is sad.

Not much we can do about it
'Cause we got a mess too—
So we hope you can do
A few things to help them.

Help My Sister

God--
We need some help for my sister
Something awful is wrong with her
I don't think the nurse knows what's wrong.
So can you show her?
We don't like to see her sick.

Maybe They Needs Help

God—
We is thankful for people
What helps us and don't always
Try to boss us around and thinks
That we got a few brains too.

We don't like the muggers and
People like that.
And we don't like the rumbles
And people who get mad easy.
We don't like the winos
What sleeps in the hall
And make a mess on the floor.

Maybe they needs some help
And maybe you will help them too.
So who knows?
Maybe they likes people
Who helps them and don't say it.

Thanks, God, for helping people.

Too Many People Sick

Things don't go so well for us, God,
Too much meanness around
And too many people sick
Maybe from pot
Or booze
Or just don't caring
Hope you do.

The Problem of Suffering

God, if you is a father
We sure need you—
'Cause we is down
And need to get up.

And they is lots of sick people
Who needs you, too!

And why does they have to be sick—
And have no job
And have a worker
To check them?

And why don't you
Do something about it?

We don't say that to be smart, God—
Only 'cause we want
To get things fixed up
If we can.

I Like Him

Jesus—
Why do people poke fun at retards?
They ain't kooks—
And even the headshrinker
Don't got help for them.
I don't like to beat the jokers up
When they do it,
But somebody's got to learn them.
And besides the kid's got to
Have somebody stand for him.
I'm glad I like him.

Griping

Dear Jesus—
We all the time griping
About the teachers,
And the guys at the school—

We forget maybe
They got a gripe about us—

So maybe if you'll help us
Take a look at us
Maybe we don't got
Such a good reason
To gripe about the other guy—

See what I mean?

Thanks, God

Thanks, God, for the parks
And the air what don't stink
And not filled with smoke
And for the grass that don't
Have lots of broken glass in it.

Thanks, God, for a place to have fun
And for the swimming pool
With clean water
And for the flowers what grows there.

Money

God, we need some money
At our house, 'cause we
Ain't got some.
Then maybe we could have
A Merry Christmas.

Help Mom

Mom is always sick
I wish you could help her
She is always bugged about something
And gets mad too quick
Maybe she drinks too much—
Can you help with that, God?

Directions, Please

God, help us to face up to what
We don't like
And help us prove a few things too.

When kids bug us to do a bad thing—
Tell us get out of there.

And if we don't
We hope you won't hold it
Against us,
And forgive us.

Learnin'

God, we ain't much at learnin'
And we don't like school
Or people always tellin' us what
To do—mostly people who
Like to boss you around too much.

Now that we is here
Maybe they got a point.

So maybe we need to learn
A few things.

Tomorrow

Dear God—Tomorrow I'm going home
I got big ideas now—
Mostly good ones like squares have—
So when the going gets rough
And the gang wants to mock me out
I'm going to need you to help me.

Please, God, when they call me chicken
And them other things I hope I get
Strong not to give a care.

Help me to think straight
And fight hard
And do what's right.

Help me think about this place
So I'll not come back.

Everybody says I will—
So I'm gonna need your help.

A Prayer for Making Right Choices

God, please help us from doing stupid things.
Why don't you make us stand up for the right
thing? When you ain't got no place to play a
ball game, or tag, it's easy to get into a mess
even if you didn't want to. Hope you will remember that. When you don't have many friends
and you are trying to get one it's easy to do what
he wants you to. Hope you'll remember that, too.
So help us, please, to do the right thing and we
will be thankful to you.

It Seems Good, Lord

Thanks for Camp Vick
Mostly for the good food
And the fun
And stuff like that
And 'cause people like you.

It seems good, Lord,
'Cause nobody's kid is crying
And 'cause they is no drunks here.

It seems good, Lord,
'Cause they is no noise
And big trucks backfiring.
So, thanks, Lord.

About Being Lazy

God, help us to stop being lazy and just hanging around. Help us to do our homework even if the other kids laugh at us for doing it. We confess that sometimes it would not take as much time to do the work as it takes to think up ways to get out of it. O God, don't let us be a dropout.

Learn Me How

Lord, I don't know all the big words the preacher sez. I ain't much at talkin' to people and tell them what I'm thinkin', but I'm in a mess now and need to know how to talk to you. I hope you will learn me how.

Grace at Meals

God, thanks for everything you can think of.

* * *

This ain't such a hot day, God,
But the food looks good.
Thanks.

* * *

God, help us to like the food we don't like.

* * *

Dear God, we give thanks
For the government surplus stuff too!

* * *

God, thanks for teeth to chew this food
Thanks for food to chew, too!

* * *

Dear God, help us
To remember people without food
Even if we don't want
To think about it when we are eatin'.

* * *

May this food help us to have big muscles
May you help us to be real good in using them
But help us to have a big heart too!

Invocations

Well, here we are again, God!
Glad to have you with us
Hope you're glad to have us.

$*$ $*$ $*$

God, we want to say great things
In our heart, mouth, and mind,
Even if it don't come out that way.

$*$ $*$ $*$

Dust us off, but good, Lord,
So we can be clean enough
For you to see.

$*$ $*$ $*$

We hope you'll be here in our church
'Cause we got nothing but good
Things to say about you.

Benedictions

God can do more than you think
He can or even the heart
You got to ask him.
Even 'til every thing is done.

     *   *   *

Now the God who never gets mad
Who helped Jesus get out of the graveyard
The one who watches over you
Who never breaks his word
Who helps you in everything
Will always be with you.

     *   *   *

God won't let you down
But will get you in
And be glad about it.
He is wise
And saves us
And there is nothing—
But nothing, man!
He can't do.

     *   *   *

Thanks, God, this has been a good day
Not one rotten thing happened today
Thanks, God.

The Psalms

The Psalms have been a source of inspiration for thousands of years. They have been used for public and private prayer, often in the form of liturgy or doxologies. The ancient writers expressed in them deep feelings of personal need and a search for answers. The Psalms also give voice to the concerns of sin, social sickness, and the overwhelming sense of lostness.

Underneath each of these cries comes the longing to find God and his love—to seek his pardon and forgiveness.

The following paraphrases of Psalms speak the same feelings, can be used the same way. Underneath the roughness of language there is still the call to God.

Hear Me When I Yell

Psalm 3

Seems like everybody is against me, God,
And people saying, "He ain't no good anyway
And nobody can do nothin' for him."

But, God, I hope you will stick by me
And hold me up when the going gets rough
And hear me when I yell for you.

On account of I'm sure
You will stick by me when I sleep
And when I'm awake
Then I won't be scared of nothin' nor nobody
No matter how many they is against me.

Deliver me, God,
'Cause I know you can bust 'em right in the face
If they bother me
And knock out their teeth
If ya have to.
We know you don't hafta very often
And we're glad.
'Cause we need your good luck more.

How About Helpin' Me Out?

Psalm 6

Dear God, don't get sore at me
And blast me out when you're mad.
Treat me cool, Lord,
'Cause I'm feeling pretty miserable inside of me
Even me bones ache
And I'm all shook up inside of me.

How about helpin' me out, God,
Before it's too late.
'Cause if I'm gone I sure can't remember you
And sing church songs.

Even I'm getting tired of faulting
All the time
And crying at night when it's still
And getting the pillow all wet.
It's even get hard to see
Anything good 'cause all I ever see is lousy
   things.

If you will only hear me, Lord,
Maybe all the bad things will go away.
Help me to get rid of guys who get me in trouble
And to believe you hear me crying
And to believe you hear me
And my prayers.

Then they will be sorry
That they was bugging me
And get out of here
And leave me alone.

Help Me Outta This Mess

Psalm 7

O God, I need to turn to you
'Cause everybody is after me again
And I need you to get out of this mess
Before I get beat up on and thrown out
When there is no one around to help me.

God, if I hurt someone
And if I was wrong
Or if I stuck up for my friend when he was
    wrong
And beat up my enemy when he was right
Then let him get me in a fair one.

But if I'm right
Then maybe you can get mad too
And we'll get the enemy together.
Let our whole gang get around you
And you can be our boss man.
Then you can size me up, God,
'Cause you sure know how to do it.
Then you can figure out my good side
'Cause I got some in me.

We put up with enough bad stuff
And it's about time you let it come to an end,
    God,
We is had enough.
But no matter what,
We still will trust you
'Cause we know that
You can size up things right.

If a man doesn't get sorry for what he has
    done
He better watch out
God's got better weapons than he has
And that man's sure to lose.
A bad guy is always thinking up a job to pull
And stupid stuff to do like breaking windows
And keeps giving people snow jobs.
This kind of stuff is no good
'Cause he only gets it in the end
When it catches up with him.

But we will give thanks to God
And give him a song.

Stick By Me, God
Psalm 54

Save me, God,
And stick by me 'cause you are so strong
I got lots of things to say to you, God,
So pay attention to what I say.

A bunch of smart alecks have ganged up on me
And are out to get me
And they don't pay no attention to God.

But I don't worry 'cause God's my helper
And sticks by me.
God will get even with my enemies
And I can trust him to end it all.

Don't worry, God, I'll pay you back somehow
And I sure thank you for helping out.
And taking care of my troubles.

We'll Call Ya When We're Bugged, Lord

Psalm 61

Don't you ever hear me crying, God,
And hear what I got to say?
Wherever we are we call ya
When we are all bugged up about something.

Help me be something better than I am
So I can have more hope
And be very strong
When I should be.

I'll try to live where you do
So you can watch me.

God, you know what I want and need
And gives something to live for
To those that trust you.

We hope you will give a long life
To people we like
And we may always remember them
'Cause they were good.
Help them to live like you want them to
And let all your good things protect them.

Then we will know we can trust you
And do what you want us to do.

We Is Still Friends, Lord

Psalm 86

Put your ear next to me, Lord,
I just want you to hear me and talk to me
'Cause I ain't got much.
Just remember I try to be like you
You are my man
So I ask for your help.
Make me happy when I'm mixed up inside.
We know you don't hold nothing against us
And you listen and hear us when we talk to you
And don't push us away.
So when we got troubles
We can call up you.

Help us remember you is only one
And everybody was made by you
And had sure better know it
And you are the only God.
Show me the right side of the street to walk on
So I can walk with you and even trust you
And not be afraid to say it
'Cause your love is just great.

When it seems like everybody is against me
And nothing goes right
And people is out to get me
Help me to know we is still friends
And that your love is here.
That's what helps me have heart.
So "give me some skin," Lord,
Then everybody will know where we stand.

You Been Around a Long Time
Psalm 90

God, you been around a long time
Even before hills and
Trees and stuff like that
You just always been God.

You make and bust men
And tell them where to go
A thousand years is nothing to you.

You can take care of bad guys
Just like they never was,
Or didn't last even a day.

We can get hurt if you get mad
And we just can't hide anything from you.
We know you check us out real good-like.

So even if we get to join the Golden Ages
You still know us
And even that just ain't much time with you
And they is gone too.

So, God, teach us to wise up
And get groovie.

Then, God, help us to hope you have pity on
        us—
And we will know your love is around in the
        morning.

Help us to get happy real soon.
And let everything go pretty good
From now to forever.

A Cheer for God!
Psalm 117

Everybody give the Lord a cheer
Everywhere in the world.
Tell the good things about Him
(They ain't no bad things anyway.)
His love is just great!
And is strong and for sure
And it lasts longer than red bricks.
Give a cheer for the Lord.

Waiting to Hear From God
Psalm 130

When I down low I turn to you, O Lord,
I sure hope you hear me
And you got me tuned in.

If you kept up with all the sins,
Who could stand up?
So I'm sure glad you hear me say, "I give."

So I'm waiting to hear from you more than
    anything

So I'm hoping for the best
And know about your love
And that you got plenty of it
(And that's a good thing, too!)

So we got nothing to worry about
Even when I'm feeling low.

Wash Us Up Real Good

Psalm 51:1—4, 9—12

God, everybody says you is good
And have a real cool for people
Who done things.

Wash us up real good
'Cause we know we didn't
Do what you want.

We know, too, we hurt you pretty bad
So we hope you won't notice
(But we know you do anyway.)

* * *

So how about making us clean
And feel good about it.
And don't kick us out,
But keep us always around you.
Then we can say we is real sorry
And mean it.

Help!

Psalm 130

When I'm beat, I need you, Lord,
So I hope you hear me
If you keep the score who could beat you?
But we don't think you will forget to
Hear us ask you for help.

So we just wait for you
To make us feel better inside.

Thanks for Standin' Up for Us

Psalm 91:1—6

God, please stick around with us
All of the time
And take good care of us.

When we need someone to
Stand up for us
We know you are ready
So we don't worry about that
And we is cool about it, God.

We are glad, too, that you won't
Let anyone beat up on us—
And protect us
Without having to kick in
So we is saying thanks, God.

Interpreting Traditional Prayers

We have long used the paraphrase as a method of Bible study, but when we tried it with prayers from the hymnals of several denominations, it was not very effective. If one examines carefully our traditional prayers, he will find that most of them give thanks for our good fortune, for blue skies, for hills and dales, for "God's great out-of-doors." It is difficult to translate these ideas into the world of the "junkie" and "wino," the poor and disenfranchised, the asphalt playground covered with broken glass.

Again we are involved in cultural and value systems that were so different that we had difficulty finding an area of common agreement from which to begin.

You're On To Us

An Invocation From the Gregorian Sacramentary
of the Seventh Century

*Almighty God, unto whom all hearts are open,
all desires known and from whom no secrets are
hid: Cleanse the thoughts of our hearts by the
inspiration of thy Holy Spirit that we may per-
fectly love thee and worthily magnify thy Holy
Name; Through Christ our Lord.*

God, we can't con you
You're on to what we think
So clean us up
Then what we say will be square
And we will live on the level.
May Christ help us to do this.

Help Us Know More

A Prayer of St. Chrysostom

Almighty God, who has given us grace at this time with one accord to make our common supplications unto thee, and dost promise that where two or three are gathered in thy name, thou wilt grant their requests, fulfill now, O Lord, the desires and petitions of thy servants, as may be most expedient for them, granting us in this world knowledge of thy truth, and in the world to come, life everlasting.

God, who says its OK to talk to him
And tells us we don't need to have
A big gang around to pray
But will always listen to us
And help us get what's good for us
And to know more
About what we suppose to know.

Give Us a Real Cool

A Prayer for Inner Peace

O God, from whom all holy desires, all good counsels, and all just works do proceed, give unto thy servants that peace which the world cannot give, that our hearts may be set to obey thy commandments, and also that we, being defended from the fear of our enemies, may by thy protection pass our time in peace and quietness; through Jesus Christ our Lord.

God, who gives us good ideas
And shows the right way
And good things get going—
Give us a real cool
So we will do what you say
And so you will stick up for us,
And so you will take care of us.

We Got Things Messed Up

Prayer of Confession

*Almighty and most merciful Father, we have
erred and strayed from thy ways like lost sheep.
We have followed too much the devices and desires of our own hearts. We have offended
against thy holy laws. We have left undone
those things which we ought to have done, and
we have done those things which we ought not
to have done. But thou, O Lord, have mercy
upon us. Spare thou those, O God, who confess
their sins. Restore thou those who are penitent,
according to thy promises declared unto man-
kind in Christ Jesus our Lord.*

God, who sure loves us,
We sure got things messed up
And are running all over the place
On account we always want to be the wheel.
We don't pay no attention to your laws
They is lots of things we didn't do
And should have
And did we shouldn't
But be good to us, God, cause
We did mean it
And after all we are telling you
About it like we oughta
So we know you will take
It easy with us—right!

Everybody's Got the Same Father

An Interpretation of the Lord's Prayer

Our Father

This says everybody's got the same father. The trouble is they ain't bright enough to know it.

Who art in heaven

That's where God lives, but if you look around here you just might get some idea what it's like even if things is a mess. Even if people act like they don't know it.

Hallowed be thy name

Means you better watch out how you use God's name and no more mockin' it out, and it still is a pretty good name even if you use it for swearin', so knock it off.

Thy kingdom come

Things is gonna get better. It's kinda hard to believe but they is. So a good place to start is with you, and me, too.

Thy will be done on earth as it is in heaven

Boy, that would sure be great if it was, man, but it ain't, so that's why we gotta go on asking and hoping that somebody will get the message.

Give us this day our daily bread

This means that we hope we can get three squares a day. Even if it is government surplus stuff.

And forgive us our debts

When we do bad things we forget it and we're sorry.

As we forgive our debtors

Forget it when someone plays you dirty. Even when we don't want to do it. 'Cause if you don't, you don't get it either.

And lead us not into temptation

Could mean don't follow the gang and get into a mess, or stand up strong.

But deliver us from evil

Means get the hell out of doing things you please and start doing the right thing.

For thine is the kingdom

Everything belongs to God even if it is hard to think so.

And the power

Means God's real strong and you can figure on him.

And the glory

Means God's just great that's all.

Forever and ever

God's so great, man, that he just never gonna end.

Amen.

That's that.

Litanies

The use of the litany as a teaching tool in Christian education is well established.

We have tried to prepare them in language that has meaning to those who participate in the worship services. Our objective here was to encourage the expression of real felt human need.

One advantage of this method is brevity. Many of the coauthors found it impossible to construct long sentences or express their thoughts in more than just a few words.

We Is Sorry, God

That we don't think much about you
  We is sorry, God.
That we used your name wrong
  We is sorry, God.
That we make believe we don't care about you
  We is sorry, God.
That we think it's big stuff to do
  We is sorry, God.
That we poke fun at people who go to church
  We is sorry, God.
That we done did it so much
  We is sorry, God.
That we waited so long to say we is sorry
  We is sorry, God.
That we hate your mercy
  We is sorry, God.
That we forget your love
  We is sorry, God.
For being too big
  We is sorry, God.
For not findin' out about you
  We is sorry, God.
For fightin' you
  We is sorry, God.
For being tough about you
  We is sorry, God.
For thinkin' we is all alone
  We is sorry, God.
For the times we said, "Who needs God?"
  We is sorry, God.
For all that kinda stuff
  We is sorry, God.

A Litany for a Happy Home

LEADER: We want some peace and quiet just for once.

CATS: That's right.

LEADER: And no fights just for once.

CATS: That's right.

LEADER: And a whole day without Mommy yellin'.

CATS: That's right, Lord.

LEADER: And Father at home, too.

CATS: That's right, Lord.

LEADER: And not at the gin mill.

CATS: That's right, Lord.

LEADER: Parents who help us and not fight each other.

CATS: That's for sure, Lord.

LEADER: Not so many kids sleeping in the same bed.

CATS: You can't sleep so good that way, Lord.

LEADER: A house without so many smashed windows will help.

CATS: It's cold that way, Lord.

LEADER: Shades that work at the window.

CATS: It's dark in the daytime, Lord.

LEADER: Parents that will listen sometimes.

CATS: Even if only once, Lord.

LEADER: A house without so much stink.

CATS: Yes, Lord.

LEADER: Just a few days of gettin' along together will help.

CATS: Too much yellin' at home, Lord.

LEADER: Help us to make these things come true, Lord.

CATS: Guess we need your help. Things are a mess now, Lord.

LEADER
AND
CATS: We need your help, Lord.

A Litany for All Cats About God Caring

LEADER: We are strictly low class.

CATS: It's hard to believe you care.

LEADER: We are used to having people look down on us.

CATS: It's hard to believe you really care.

LEADER: We don't like feeling like this.

CATS: But it is hard to believe you care.

LEADER: We are used to people yellin' at us.

CATS: Why don't you yell at us too?

LEADER: We don't like doing the things that you don't like.

CATS: But we don't think you care.

LEADER: It is hard not to think of stealing when all the others have things that we don't.

CATS: We wonder if you care about us.

LEADER: You talk about love, and loving others.

CATS: We want to feel your love but we don't know how.

LEADER: We do a lot of hating but we don't really know why but we can think up lots of reasons why and stinkers to hate.

CATS: Sometimes the reasons are honest and nobody accepts us. That's why we wonder if you care about us.

LEADER: We don't want to be a phony. And we don't think we are.

CATS: We just don't think you care—but we want you to.

A Litany for Family

God, the preacher tells us we is all just one big
    family.
  So for what we got, we say
        Thanks.
For the fun at the playground
        Thanks.
For folk singers who came to see us
        Thanks.
For people what help us
        Thanks.
For people who help get others well
        Thanks.
For the center
        Thanks.
For people who like us and don't want nothing
        Thanks.
For people who shows the right way
        Thanks.

So, God, we need you to show us we need to
    belong to the family too.

A Litany About "Things We Don't Want"

From getting all mixed up
   Don't let us do it.
From only thinking of ourselves
   Don't let us do it.
From being too lazy
   Don't let us do it.
From not caring about others
   Don't let us do it.
From following the gang of other kids
   Don't let us do it.
From being scared of what they will say
   Don't let us do it.
From forgetting too many things
   Don't let us do it.
From thinking we is better than someone else
   Don't let us do it.
From always wanting to bomb around
   Don't let us do it.
From always wanting everything real boss
   Don't let us do it.
From shutting the door on you
   Don't let us do it.
From always griping
   Don't let us do it.
From too much swearing
   Don't let us do it.
From hating other people
   Don't let us do it.

A Litany for Others

God, help us give a care for others
  We ask your help.
For those what got kicked out of their houses
  We ask your help.
For those what fights for us
  We ask your help.
For those who ain't got no job
  We ask your help.
For those who give up too soon
  We ask your help.
For those who thinks that clothes is everything
  We ask your help.
For those who are always bugged by others
  We ask your help.
For those who just hang around
  We ask your help.
For those who need to try harder
  We ask your help.
For those who think they know it all
  We ask your help.
But don't know as much as they think
  We ask your help.
For those who think we are dirt
  We ask your help.
Help us, God, to give a care.

A Litany for People Who "Got Troubles"

O God, we pray for all the people we know.
  Help them out today.
We know some of them ain't so hot.
  Help them out today.
We know some of them ain't so bad either.
  Help them out today.
We hope you will get them better houses.
  Help them out today.
We hope you will get help them get a job.
  Help them out today.
We hope you will help them get a bike, too.
  Help them out today.
We hope you will help stop the fights.
  Help them out today.
We hope you will help the ones what ain't got
    parents what cares.
  Help them out today.
We hope you will help them keep houses clean.
  Help them out today.
We hope you will help them stop running away.
  Help them out today.
We hope you will help them stop using dope.
  Help them out today.
We hope you will help them pretty soon, too.
  Help them out today.

A Litany About "Not Thinking"

We ain't done so hot today, Lord.
    Please forgive us.
We wanted to be "the wheel."
    Please forgive us.
We didn't try very hard in school either.
    Please forgive us.
We didn't care either.
    Please forgive us.
We hurt ourselves.
    Please forgive us.
We spoke dirty words.
    Please forgive us.
We told a few lies
    Please forgive us.
We beat up a kid.
    Please forgive us.
We got hot too soon.
    Please forgive us.
We want to do better.
    Please help us.
We just wished we could get goin' again.
    Please help us.
We hope we don't forget.

Who'll Live in Your House?

Psalm 15

LEADER : O Lord, who shall live in your house?

PEOPLE : Who shall stick around your yard?

LEADER : The one who pulls no jobs and does right

PEOPLE : And levels with you

LEADER : And the one who plays it straight

PEOPLE : And who sticks by his friend
and don't go up on other people

LEADER : And the one who hates rotten things

PEOPLE : And who trusts God's friends.

LEADER : And who always stands true

PEOPLE : And not the loan sharks
And not the squealers.

LEADER
AND
PEOPLE : And all that's for sure
And this will always be so.

Everything Is God's

Psalm 24

LEADER: Everything is God's

PEOPLE: Even the people

LEADER: He made the world

PEOPLE: And everything in it.

LEADER: Who is going to be with God

PEOPLE: And get to stand by him?

LEADER: People who come clean

PEOPLE: And don't snow you—that's who!

LEADER: He'll get good things from God

PEOPLE: And God will stand by him, man!

LEADER: So hold up your head

PEOPLE: And open up, man!
So God can get with you.

LEADER: So who is he?

PEOPLE: The strongest of the strong, that's who

LEADER: So stand up real strong-like

PEOPLE: 'Cause God's with us.

Will Ya Be Our Helper?

Psalm 60:1—5, 11—12

LEADER: God, why did you throw us out, and all over the block?

KIDS: Why are ya mad at us? Come on back back again.

LEADER: You made the world.

KIDS: Why don't ya fix it up 'cause it's pretty bad.

LEADER: You showed the people lots of things

KIDS: And gave them lots of stuff.

LEADER: You even gave a secret sign to people who trusted ya

KIDS: So they could always win.

LEADER: So they always won.

KIDS: Help us to win too.

* * *

LEADER: When the going gets rough will ya be our helper?

KIDS: 'Cause the help we get sometimes don't help much, that is.

LEADER: From God we can do good things

KIDS: 'Cause he will keep people from hurting you.

Worship Services in Jail

The following are examples of different types of worship services that can be used to present basic values and concepts of our faith.

In some of these services you will note the absence of a sermon. We have not found a sermon to be a very effective tool of teaching in a jail setting. Perhaps the reason for this is seen in some of the original prayers. Many of the youth are being told what to do and how to do it, in some cases by inadequate parents, teachers, social workers—and many others. Many are just tired of being preached at. Our purpose, then, was to awaken interest that could lead to discussion either in small groups or in a conference with the chaplain.

We learned as time went on the importance of keeping new innovations within a time perspective. We tried to maintain ties with the past by following an "order of worship" such as might be encountered in a local church. In addition hymns of general use were worked in. The main departure from the traditional was in the use of modern music—combos, guitars, and drums. An organ was also used, again a tie with the past. Traditional spirituals, some well known and others not so familiar, were used, as were folk ballads. Music of all forms proved again to be a language that all understood. For those who may object to some of the ballads selected, my only defense is that God can speak through a current "hit" as well as through Bach.

We used *Good News for Modern Man* (published by the American Bible Society) for the Bible readings except as noted. We also discovered that it adds to interest and attention to have members of the congregation participate. They should, however, be selected carefully for their ability to read and to control their embarrassment.

The prayers and responsive sections of the services were prepared either by small groups or by individuals working with the chaplain. He selected the Scriptures and set the theme for each of the services.

Many books of folk songs that can be used are available. And the traditional forms of worship, such as the Gloria Patri and the Doxology, can also be used.

A Service to Remind Us of the Jesus Way

PRELUDE (organ and combo)

CHAPLAIN:

Today we take a look at what a Christian means by saying we follow Jesus. We all follow something—the crowd or the gang, maybe our own ideas, or maybe we just live from one day to the next, but that's following something, too—like nothing; emptiness is what some call it. So before junking the idea of following the Jesus way, at least take a look; sing the songs, listen to the prayers and Bible readings, and then—it's up to you.

SPIRITUAL: "Lonesome Valley"

INVOCATION:

We have listened to all kinds of voices and people giving advice, Lord. So far we haven't listened very much to you. Help us not only to listen, but also to hear what is being said. When we know the facts, help us to make up our own mind.

SCRIPTURE LESSON: "A Really Great Saying"
    (Mark 12:28–31)

RESPONSIVE PRAYER:

Chaplain: O Lord, we ask you to listen to us.

People: We have not let Christ into our life and now we are looking for him.

Chaplain: We at least want to respect him

People: So we can walk his way.

Chaplain: We have poked fun at his way

People: But most of the time we didn't know what we were talking about.

Chaplain: Now we really are trying to find out what it is all about

People: So we listen to you, God.

SCRIPTURE LESSON: "Just How Important Are You?" (Matthew 5:13–16)

SONG: "Blowing in the Wind"

RESPONSIVE LESSON OF QUESTIONS:

Chaplain: If we are all that important,

People: Why do we forget God?

Chaplain: Why don't we want to know about him?

People: Why are we always wanting to be "a wheel"?

Chaplain: Why don't we pray except when we are in trouble?

People: Why are we always trying to use people?

Chaplain:	Why do our good ideas backfire?
People:	Why are we so quick to blast people out?
Chaplain:	Why don't we try to put things right?
People:	How can we do that?

SCRIPTURE LESSON: "This Is How God Does It" (Romans 3:21–31)

SONG: "Climb Every Mountain"

SCRIPTURE LESSON: "This Goes for You, Too" (John 3:1–21)

CHOIR: "Standing in the Need of Prayer"

SCRIPTURE LESSON: "First Things First—Right?" (Matthew 26:33)

SPIRITUAL: "Over My Head"

BENEDICTION:

| Chaplain: | May God always be in your mind May God always be in your acts |
| People: | May we always remember this. |

POSTLUDE (organ and combo)

A Service About Forgiving and Forgetting

PRELUDE (organ and drums)

CALL TO WORSHIP:

God is here—and in the whole world everybody listens to him.

SONG: "Michael Row His Boat Ashore"

PRAYER OF CONFESSION (chaplain and people):

We have sure got things messed up and knocking around like a pack of dogs. We have only done what we wanted to do. We even pushed your laws around. There is lots of things we didn't do we should have done—and some we done we should have forgot.

But, God, please take it easy on us. Let off those who got heart to tell you about it and level with you. Give lots of strength to those who earn it and is sorry for what they did—just like you said you would. And after this, may we always do what is right.

THE LORD'S PRAYER

SCRIPTURE LESSON: "Sticking With It"
    (Philippians 3:12–18)

PRAYER HYMN: "Kum Bi Ya, Ma Lord"

Chaplain: **The Lord** be with you

People: And with thy spirit.

Chaplain: Let us pray.

PASTORAL PRAYER (in chaplain's own words)

RESPONSIVE READING:

Chaplain: God be good to us and look upon us

People: That your ways may be known to us.

Chaplain: Let people praise you, O God,

People: Let everybody everywhere be glad.

Chaplain: You, God, will judge us and rule us,

People: Let everyone praise you.

Chaplain: Then God will bless us,

People: God will bless us for sure.

SOLO: "A Cry in the Night"

CHAPLAIN'S TALK:

Did you ever get a job, but just forget to tell the boss you had a record? Everything is going real great. Then it happens—the boss finds out about it. And what you thought was done and hid pops up.

Then you feel bad. Sometimes that record keeps us awake at night or makes us feel just lousy. Some tough people keep this pushed down—or they think they do.

Forgetting is a good thing sometimes—sort of telling your conscience to shut up. Some people seem to do that, I guess; but I guess, too, that most of them who boast they can do it don't.

But what if you just can't forget and the past just keeps jumping up? Then the guy who thinks he's got the world in his hands finds he lost it and he's bugged by his thoughts. What then?

What about his wanting to feel clean? Can he ever again?

What it boils down to is this—or at least the Bible says this: We can try to forget the rotten things and dirty deals we gave people, but they still pop out and we likely never get away from them. Or we can face them, take our knocks, ask for and get forgiveness from God himself.

It's like getting the blackboard washed clean again. Anyone can try to forget, or use booze or goofballs or narcotics. Anyone can try to forget by controlling his conscience. But only God can forgive, or has the ability to forgive, to clean us up and start us again.

Being forgiven is a good thing and makes sense. It comes through believing that God's Son is your friend and guide.

FOLK SONG: "Blowing in the Wind"

BENEDICTION:

> *Chaplain:* God be with us
> *People:* Christ be with us
> *All:* Amen.

A Service About Getting Good Things

PRELUDE (organ, guitar, and harmonica) : "When The Saints Go Marchin' In"; "Domonique"

CALL TO WORSHIP:

Chaplain: God lights up men's hearts when they look for him.

People: Help us to search you out, O God.

Chaplain: Let everybody be very still

People: So we can hear God speak.

SPIRITUAL : "Amen, Amen"

INVOCATION : See page 63.

THE LORD'S PRAYER

CHOIR : "Every Time I Feel the Spirit"

CHAPLAIN'S PRAYER (his own words)

RESPONSIVE READING (based on the Beatitudes) :

Chaplain: Happy is the man who knows when he stands with God.

People: Heaven is near enough to reach.

Chaplain: Happy are those who have a great loss

People: Because God is close by.

Chaplain: Happy are those who do the right thing

People: Because God will stand by them.

Chaplain: Happy are those who care about other people

People: Because God will care about them.

Chaplain: Happy are those who follow God

People: Because they will see him.

Chaplain: Happy are those who work for peace

People: They are sons of God.

Chaplain: Happy are those who get mocked out for going God's way

People: Because God is with them.

SONG: "If I Had a Hammer"

CHAPLAIN'S TALK: Theme—"Is God Here in Jail?"

SONG: "Five Hundred Miles"

BENEDICTION

POSTLUDE (organ, guitar, and harmonica)

A Service on Living Life "For Real"

PRELUDE (organ and drums): "Lord of the Dance" (folk song); "Certainly, Lord" (spiritual); "Joyful, Joyful" (hymn)

CHAPLAIN:

"One day is as lousy as another." Did you ever think like that? Maybe feel like you wish you were never born? Some people call it being "down in the dumps," or "the blues," or "stretched out thin." Don't make much difference what you call it; it ends up the same anyway. Sometimes the thing that bugs us is, How come some people always seem to be turned on even when they don't get the breaks? Today with some songs, a few prayers, Bible readings, let's see if we can get the idea of how God can help us get over our roadblocks.

HYMN: "Fairest Lord Jesus"

INVOCATION:

When life is a mess and real gone, we ask you, O Lord, to help us find another road. The one we are on now is sure a dead end. Sometimes we think there is no use, but then we think that there just might be, so help us to listen and hear what is said today in our songs, prayers, and readings.

THE LORD'S PRAYER

SOLO: "I Walked Today Where Jesus Walked"

SCRIPTURE LESSON: "So Why Be Stretched Out Thin?" (John 16:16–24)

FOLK SONG: "Where Have All the Flowers Gone?"

SCRIPTURE LESSON: "They Goin' to Get God's Help" (The Beatitudes, Matthew 5:3–11, in part, from *God Is for Real, Man,* page 56)

RESPONSIVE LESSON:

Chaplain: God wants us to feel good

People: And to think and use our minds.

Chaplain: God wants us to walk straight

People: And to work at it.

Chaplain: God wants us to rule ourselves

People: But with his help,

Chaplain: God wants us to be helpful

People: And give a person a break.

Chaplain: God knows that doing things like that

People: Makes us all feel great.

Chaplain: Let's talk to God about it.

All: Give us, we ask you, God, a new way of thinking and a new way of acting, so that, making life worth living for someone else, we may find life for us, too.

CHOIR: "There Is a New Name in Glory" (congregation keeps time with hand claps)

SCRIPTURE LESSON: "They Were Real Important-Like" (Jesus Call His Disciples, John 1:35–51, from *God Is for Real, Man,* page 86)

SONG: "Jacob's Ladder"

SCRIPTURE LESSON: "So Why Worry?" (II Corinthians 4:1–18)

SOLO: "Balm in Gilead"

SCRIPTURE LESSON: "Button Up, Man" (Ephesians 6:10–18)

HYMN: "Are Ye Able"

PRAYER OF BENEDICTION (chaplain and people):

Now, Lord, we ask you to make us strong; and for courage to be the kind of people we already know we should be.

A Chapel Service on "Standing Up Straight"

PRELUDE (organ and guitar): "Love Divine" (hymn); "Balm in Gilead" (spiritual)

SPIRITUAL: "Go, Tell It on the Mountain"

INVOCATION (by inmate):

Our Lord, who had real heart and stood up to his enemies, make us like you. Give us a new thought and a clear sidewalk and something to shoot for. Keep us from messing our life up and not thinking straight.

SONG: "The Same Boat, Brother"

SCRIPTURE LESSON: Joshua 1:5–9

SPIRITUAL: "Lord, I Want to Be a Christian"

CHAPLAIN'S TALK: "Getting Hard Things Done First"

HYMN: "Faith of Our Fathers"

BENEDICTION

A Service of Prayer for Everybody

PRELUDE (organ, guitars, and banjo) : "If I Had a Hammer"; "What a Friend"

CALL TO WORSHIP :

> *Chaplain:* God is here in this chapel
>
> *People:* So why not listen to him?
>
> *Chaplain:* He does hear our prayers
>
> *People:* And answers them, too.

HYMN : "A Cry in the Night"

INVOCATION

THE LORD'S PRAYER

SOLO : "I Walked Today Where Jesus Walked"

"A LITANY FOR ALL CATS ABOUT GOD CARING" (see page 90)

SCRIPTURE LESSON : "Beating Out Evil" (Romans 12:1–21)

THE PRAYER FOR EVERYBODY :

> *Chaplain:* Let's pray for people who got lots of problems

For those who are scared
For people who are sick
And who are hungry
And who get up lots of hope
But nothing happens.

Silence

Chaplain: Let us pray for those who have nobody to care about them

People: This is what we are doing, Lord.

Chaplain: And for people who can't find a job

People: This is what we are doing, Lord.

Chaplain: And for people without homes

People: This is what we are doing, Lord.

Chaplain: And for those who have nothing to live for

People: This is what we are doing, Lord.

Chaplain: And for those who give up too soon

People: This is what we are doing, Lord.

Chaplain: And those who live from one fix to another

People: This is what we are doing, Lord.

Chaplain: And those who always need a drink

People: This is what we are doing, Lord.

Silence

All: Lord, we don't have much to give, and we too need help from you. If we have any faith, help us share it and what we have help us to share with others, so that we can share with you.

SCRIPTURE LESSON: "No One Is Ever Too Low" (Matthew 25:37)

SPIRITUAL: "Nobody Knows"

SCRIPTURE LESSON: "How to Use What You Have" (Matthew 25:19–28)

CHOIR: "Standing in the Need of Prayer"

SCRIPTURE LESSON: "Putting Our Acts Where Our Mouth Is" (James 2:1–17)

FOLK SONG: "If I Had a Hammer"

BENEDICTION:

Chaplain: May God go with you

People: And be with you, too

Chaplain: And stay with us forever

People: And forever

All: Amen.

POSTLUDE (organ, guitars, and banjo)

A Service of Communion

(Music for this service is from *"Joy Is Like the Rain"*
by the Medical Mission Sisters)

PRELUDE (organ, guitar, and drums)

CALL TO WORSHIP:

> *Chaplain:* Clap your hands all people,
>
> *People:* Shout to God with loud songs of joy,
>
> *Chaplain:* Because he made us,
>
> *People:* And everything else too.

HYMN: "Joy Is Like the Rain"

INVOCATION: "Give Us a Lift" (see page 41)

SOLO: "Come Down, Lord"

A LITANY FOR JAIL:

> *Chaplain:* Almighty God, who had nothing to do with our coming here, help us to remember the homes we came from—good or bad.
>
> *People:* We ask your help, O God.
>
> *Chaplain:* That we may remember the faith of those who trusted us

People: We ask your help, O God.

Chaplain: That knowing men despise us we may with courage find our self again with your help

People: We ask your help, O God.

Chaplain: From all sense of strangeness and loneliness and fear

People: We ask your help, O God.

Chaplain: From joining the crowd, from sins that call us, from bitterness

People: We ask your help, O God.

Chaplain: From forgetting chances we had from distrust of our self

People: We ask your help, O God.

Chaplain: From failing to use this time to consider our motive

People: We ask your help, O God.

Chaplain: From failing to develop a clear conscience

People: We ask your help, O God.

THE GLORIA PATRI

GOSPEL LESSON: "Throwin' a Party for Junior" (The Prodigal Son's Return, Luke 15:11–22, from *God Is for Real, Man,* page 82)

HYMN: "Pilgrim Song" (guitar accompaniment only)

PRAYER:

Chaplain: Let's talk to God

People: It'll be good to listen too!

Chaplain: Tell him all that is bugging you

People: But don't forget to listen too.

Chaplain: Let us pray to God. (Chaplain prays in his own words or reads a selection from this book.)

RESPONSE (organ, guitar, and drums)

CHAPLAIN'S WORD: Theme—"Turning to God Is Joy"

HYMN FOR COMMUNION: "God Gives His People Strength"

GIVING OF THE BREAD

SOLO: "How I Have Longed"

GIVING OF THE CUP

HYMN: "Spirit of God"

BENEDICTION:

Chaplain: May God's blessings be with all of you.

People: And with you too.

All: May God's quietness,
His love
His care
His hope
Be with all of us.

POSTLUDE: Replay music used in the service.

Daily Devotions

The basic purpose of each of these "daily devotions," or "talks with God," was to raise a question of doubt, but never to lecture. Sometimes this provided the springboard to a fuller discussion of the issues involved. The discussions became the pathway for a person learning that he too could talk with God, or at least for an earnest confrontation with prayer, even if it was rejected.

First Day

SOMETHING TO THINK ABOUT:

What and who really brought you here?

SOMETHING TO READ:

"Finding God" (Acts 3:13–26)

SOMETHING MORE TO THINK ABOUT:

Most everybody has some darkness he goes through. Maybe this is yours. So you're in jail —and I say, "So what!" That may seem way out—knowing what you're facing, like a bit in the pen—but still I say, "So what?" That's just a way of saying again that it's not like the end.

A PRAYER:

From all the very foolish acts I've done, O God, deliver me and build a real cool in me. Help me to figure things out right.

Second Day

SOMETHING TO THINK ABOUT:
So what do we do about it?

SOMETHING TO READ:
Matthew 6:24–34

SOMETHING MORE TO THINK ABOUT:
Can't find the right street ... signpost is missing ... maybe some kids broke it. More than that, the streetlight's out, too, so you wander around and end up on the same street you started on ... so what do you do? Most of the time you ask someone who knows the way. A long time ago a fellow, named Thomas, was pretty mixed up too. When he asked the way Christ said to him, "I am the Way."

A PRAYER:
When we lose sight of you
Help us to ask people who know your way.
Then we, too, can know it.

Third Day

SOMETHING TO THINK ABOUT:
Who's the boss?

SOMETHING TO READ:
"Bugging" (James 1)

SOMETHING MORE TO THINK ABOUT:
You know who the boss is in the life of a junkie—or a wino? It's dope and booze. But everybody's got a boss—of some kind—like never being able to make up our mind or being scared of what friends will think or even just not caring. Lots of other things we could list—so who's your boss?

A PRAYER:
God be in my head and in my understanding;
God be in my eyes and in my looking;
God be in my mouth and in my speaking;
God be in my heart and in my thinking.

Fourth Day

What's courage?

II Timothy 2:1–26

Lots of people talk about it and how important it is. Call it lots of names too—like "guts"
and "heart" and many other words. I don't
care what you call it, but it sure takes a lot
of it to stay out of this jail and not much to
get in.

A PRAYER:

God, help us stand up like a man
Teach us when to say No
And Yes—and make it stick.

Fifth Day

SOMETHING TO THINK ABOUT:
What's right?

SOMETHING TO READ:
Psalm 51

SOMETHING MORE TO THINK ABOUT:
What would happen if everybody did what I do? Thought like I do? Go ahead, answer that question—see where it leaves you. Or maybe you can ask yourself, What's really going to happen to me if I keep going down this road? Is it a dead end? What's happening to my family—because of me? Most people believe life comes from God. Why waste it?

A PRAYER:
O God, wake up our thoughts
And give us courage
To be the kind of people
We know we ought to be.

Sixth Day

SOMETHING TO THINK ABOUT:
Where does real strength come from?

SOMETHING TO READ:
Psalm 46

SOMETHING MORE TO THINK ABOUT:
We all got our weak points. Some people have it in health—like always catching a cold—or being sick some other way. Some people are weak in making up their own minds—most of the time letting someone else tell them what to do. Some people are always running away from something—never standing up on their own feet and facing the gaff—and doing something about it.

A PRAYER:
O God, we hear lots of people talking—
Help us to talk to you.
When you answer—may we get strength
To see ourself as we ought to be.

Seventh Day

SOMETHING TO THINK ABOUT:
Is God's love here?

SOMETHING TO READ:
Psalm 23
John 3:1–16

SOMETHING MORE TO THINK ABOUT:
Sure there is lots of hate and just plain dirt in the world. Lots of people got it real rough and lots more people are hurt that shouldn't be. There's lots more that could be said on that, too. But there is the other side, just like there is heads and tails on a dime. Why do you suppose people give time to help out in hospitals—or at the community house—or help send kids to summer camps—or teach at a church? They don't have to do it, you know.

A PRAYER:
O God, help me
To look and see
And listen and hear.
Help me to figure things out right.

Glossary

BIG MAN : important person
BIT : jail sentence
BOSS : in style
BUG : to disturb ; to bother
BUSTED : arrested

CATS : people, girl or man
CHICKEN : fearful ; one who is afraid
CLIMBING UP ON : fighting
COOL : slow and easy
CREEPS : strange persons
CRIB : home

FLAGGED OUT : failed
FUZ : police
FUZ WAGON : squad car

GAFF : bad news
GETTING HIT : being sent to prison
GET WITH IT : try harder
GIVE ME SOME SKIN : shake hands with me
GROOVE : on the right track ; something good

HEADSHRINKER : psychiatrist
HEART : willingness to fight

I GIVE : an acknowledgment of defeat

KNOCK IT OFF: stop

LAME: weak

MAKE IT: to succeed
MOCK OUT: poke fun at; ridicule
MUGGER: robber
MY MAN: a favorite person

ON THE LOOSE: describes one with no family

PEN: penitentiary
POT: marihuana
PUNT OUT: to go too far
PUSHED DOWN: feeling very beat

RETARD: a mentally retarded person
RUMBLE: a gang fight

SNOW JOB: group of lies
SQUEALER: one who tells on others
STRETCHED OUT: feeling sad

TEACH: schoolteacher
TUNED IN: listening

WINO: drunk
WORKER: social caseworker